Corrections
Situation Judgement
Practice Workbook

Complete
Test Preparation Inc.
WWW.TEST-PREPARATION.CA

COPYRIGHT

Copyright © 2024
Complete Test Preparation Inc. ALL RIGHTS RESERVED.

No part of this book may be reproduced or transferred in any form or by any means, graphic, electronic, or mechanical, including photocopying, recording, web distribution, taping, or by any information storage retrieval system, without the written permission of the author.

Notice: Complete Test Preparation Inc. makes every reasonable effort to obtain from reliable sources accurate, complete, and timely information about the tests covered in this book. Nevertheless, changes can be made in the tests or the administration of the tests at any time. Complete Test Preparation Inc. make no representations or warranties of any kind, express or implied, about the completeness, accuracy, reliability, suitability or availability with respect to the information contained in this document for any purpose. Any reliance you place on such information is therefore strictly at your own risk.

The author(s) shall not be liable for any loss incurred as a consequence of the use and application, directly or indirectly, of any information presented in this work. Sold with the understanding, the author is not engaged in rendering professional services or advice. If advice or expert assistance is required, the services of a competent professional should be sought.

The company, product and service names used in this publication are for identification purposes only. All trademarks and registered trademarks are the property of their respective owners.

Complete Test Preparation Inc. is not affiliated with, or endorsed by Canada Corrections.

We strongly recommend that students check with exam providers for up-to-date information regarding test content.

This product is provided for skill practice only

ISBN-13: 9781772454451

Version 8.5 Updated December 2024

Company Overview

Why Us?
The Complete Test Preparation Team has been publishing high quality study materials since 2005, with a catalogue of over 175 test prep titles, in, as well as ESL textbooks and online classes for all levels.

To keep up with the industry changes, we update everything all the time!

Available in all formats

- Amazon paperback
- Independent bookstores
- Kindle
- Books
- Google Play
- Kobo
- Online Courses
- PDF Download

Languages

- English
- French
- Spanish
- Chinese

And the best part?

With every purchase, you're helping people all over the world improve themselves and their education. So thank you in advance for supporting this mission with us! Together, we are truly making a difference in the lives of those often forgotten by the system.

Charities that we support
https://www.test-preparation.ca/charities-and-non-profits/

You have definitely come to the right place.
If you want to spend your valuable study time where it will help you the most - we've got you covered today and tomorrow.

Feedback

We welcome your feedback. Email us at feedback@test-preparation.ca with your comments and suggestions. We carefully review all suggestions and often incorporate reader suggestions into upcoming versions. As a Print on Demand Publisher, we update our products frequently.

https://www.facebook.com/CompleteTestPreparation/

https://www.youtube.com/user/MrTestPreparation

CONTENTS

8 **GETTING STARTED**
About the Corrections Situation Judgement Test — 9

11 **CORRECTIONS SITUATION JUDGMENT QUIZ 1**
Answer Key — 30

38 **CORRECTIONS SITUATION JUDGMENT QUIZ 2**
Answer Key — 50

55 **DILEMMA AND JUDGEMENT ANALYSIS 1**
RESPONSE TO FIRE — 55

58 **DILEMMA AND JUDGEMENT ANALYSIS 2**
ENSURING SAFETY — 58

61 **DILEMMA AND JUDGEMENT ANALYSIS 3**
BALANCING INMATE ACCOUNTABILITY — 61

64 **DILEMMA AND JUDGEMENT ANALYSIS 4**
SECURITY OF INMATES — 64

67 **DILEMMA AND JUDGEMENT ANALYSIS 4**
SECURITY OF INMATES DURING TRANSPORT — 67

70 **HOW TO PREPARE FOR A TEST**

75 **HOW TO TAKE A TEST**
- Reading the Instructions — 75
- How to Take a Test - The Basics — 76
- In the Test Room – What you MUST do! — 81
- Avoid Anxiety Before a Test — 86
- Common Test-Taking Mistakes — 88

91 **CONCLUSION**

92 **ONLINE RESOURCES**

Getting Started

Congratulations! By deciding to take the Corrections Situation Judgement Test, you have taken the first step toward a great future! Of course, there is no point in taking this important exam unless you intend to do your best to earn the highest grade you possibly can. That means getting yourself organized and discovering the best approaches, methods and strategies to master the material. Yes, that will require real effort and dedication on your part, but if you are willing to focus your energy and devote the study time necessary, before you know it you will be on you way to a brighter future.

We know that taking on a new endeavour can be scary, and it is easy to feel unsure of where to begin. That's where we come in. This practice workbook is designed to help you improve your situational judgment and test-taking skills, show you a few tricks of the trade and increase your competency and confidence.

Getting Started

About the Corrections Situation Judgement Test

The Corrections Situational Judgment Test (SJT) is a critical component in the selection process for correctional officers, designed to assess candidates' judgment and decision-making abilities in real-life scenarios.

Purpose and Importance

The primary objective of the Corrections SJT is to evaluate how you handle complex, and often high-pressure situations a corrections officer would likely encounter everyday. This assessment ensures that prospective officers possess the necessary competencies to maintain safety, security, and order within institutions.

Test Structure

The test presents a series of hypothetical scenarios. Each scenario is followed by multiple-choice responses, where candidates must select the most appropriate action. The scenarios typically cover:

> **Response to Emergencies:** Handling fires, environmental hazards, or medical crises.
> **Security Management:** Ensuring the safety of the institution, public, and inmates, including during transport.
> **Offender Accountability:** Promoting and enforcing responsible behavior among inmates.

These themes align with the core functions and expectations of correctional officers, providing a realistic preview of the challenges they may face.

Competencies

The Corrections SJT evaluates several key competencies such as:

Integrity and Respect: Upholding ethical standards and treating all individuals with dignity.
Critical Thinking: Analyzing situations thoroughly to make informed decisions.
Teamwork: Collaborating effectively with colleagues to achieve common goals.
Initiative and Action Orientation: Pro-actively addressing issues and taking decisive actions when necessary.
Effective Communication: Conveying information clearly and listening actively to others.

Quick Study Tips

Here's a short and effective list for studying and practicing for a test:

Practice Regularly: Complete practice questions or mock tests to improve familiarity and identify weak areas.

Review Mistakes: Analyze incorrect answers to understand your errors and learn from them.

Focus on Key Skills: Target the specific competencies or knowledge areas the test emphasizes.

Take Breaks: Incorporate short breaks to maintain focus and avoid burnout.

Quiz 1

Test Overview:

This assessment presents a series of hypothetical, work-related scenarios. Each scenario is followed by possible responses. Your task is to evaluate these responses based on their effectiveness in addressing the given situation.

Response Selection:

For each scenario, you will be asked to:

Select the Most Effective Response: Choose the option you believe best resolves or manages the situation.

Answering Guidelines:

- Base your judgments on the information provided in each scenario.
- Consider best practices, ethical standards, and professional behavior relevant to the role.
- There are no "trick" questions; focus on practical and appropriate actions.
- Read each scenario and its corresponding responses carefully before making selections.
- Ensure you understand the context and nuances of each situation.

Corrections Situation Judgement

Answer Sheet

	A	B	C	D	E		A	B	C	D	E
1	○	○	○	○	○	21	○	○	○	○	○
2	○	○	○	○	○	22	○	○	○	○	○
3	○	○	○	○	○	23	○	○	○	○	○
4	○	○	○	○	○	24	○	○	○	○	○
5	○	○	○	○	○	25	○	○	○	○	○
6	○	○	○	○	○	26	○	○	○	○	○
7	○	○	○	○	○	27	○	○	○	○	○
8	○	○	○	○	○	28	○	○	○	○	○
9	○	○	○	○	○	29	○	○	○	○	○
10	○	○	○	○	○	30	○	○	○	○	○
11	○	○	○	○	○	31	○	○	○	○	○
12	○	○	○	○	○	32	○	○	○	○	○
13	○	○	○	○	○	33	○	○	○	○	○
14	○	○	○	○	○	34	○	○	○	○	○
15	○	○	○	○	○	35	○	○	○	○	○
16	○	○	○	○	○	36	○	○	○	○	○
17	○	○	○	○	○	37	○	○	○	○	○
18	○	○	○	○	○	38	○	○	○	○	○
19	○	○	○	○	○	39	○	○	○	○	○
20	○	○	○	○	○	40	○	○	○	○	○

Quiz 1

1. Scenario: An Unauthorized Entry Attempt
Situation: While on duty, you notice an individual attempting to gain unauthorized access to the building.
Question: What should be your immediate response in this situation?

    a. Confront the individual and demand identification

    b. Ignore the individual and continue with your duties.

    c. Escort the individual out of the premises.

    d. Secure the area and notify the appropriate authorities.

2. Scenario: Emergency Lock-down Procedure
Situation: A major security breach has occurred, requiring the implementation of an emergency lock-down.
Question: What should be your immediate response in this situation?

    a. Evacuate the facility and seek assistance from external authorities.

    b. Inform staff members and initiate the lock-down procedure.

    c. Attempt to apprehend the individuals responsible for the breach.

    d. Continue regular activities and ignore the security breach.

3. Scenario: Tracking Offender Compliance

Situation: As a corrections officer, you are responsible for tracking the compliance of offenders with their assigned programs and activities. One offender consistently fails to attend mandatory counseling sessions.
Question: What should be your immediate response in this situation?

>   a. Ignore the non-compliance and hope the offender improves.
>
>   b. Reduce the level of supervision for the offender.
>
>   c. Document the non-compliance and report it to the supervisor.
>
>   d. Provide a verbal warning to the offender.

4. Scenario: Suspicious Package
Situation: During a routine inspection, you discover a suspicious package in a public area of the institution.
Question: What should be your immediate response in this situation?

>   a. Examine the exterior of the package closely.
>
>   b. Disregard the package and continue with your inspection.
>
>   c. Evacuate the area and inform the appropriate authorities.
>
>   d. Open the package to investigate its contents.

5. Scenario: Disturbance in the Visitation Area
Situation: While monitoring the visitation area, you witness a heated argument between an inmate and their visitor.
Question: What should be your immediate response in this situation?

    a. Call for backup and request assistance from fellow officers.

    b. Ignore the situation and allow it to resolve on its own.

    c. Escort the visitor out of the facility immediately.

    d. Intervene physically to separate the individuals involved.

6. Scenarios: Monitoring Rule Violations
Situation: While conducting routine inspections, you observe an offender engaging in unauthorized communication with another offender, which violates facility rules.
Question: What should be your immediate response in this situation?

    a. Overlook the violation as long as it doesn't escalate.

    b. Report the rule violation to the appropriate authorities.

    c. Inform other staff members, but take no further action.

    d. Confront the offenders and administer disciplinary measures.

7. Scenario: Encouraging Positive Behavior
Situation: An offender consistently demonstrates positive behavior and actively participates in rehabilitative programs.
Question: What should be your immediate response in this situation?

    a. Assign additional responsibilities to the offender.

    b. Ignore the positive behavior as it is expected.

    c. Reduce supervision and monitoring for the offender.

    d. Acknowledge and praise the offender for their efforts.

Corrections Situation Judgement

8. Scenario: Addressing Non-Compliance
Situation: An offender consistently violates facility rules by engaging in contraband activities.
Question: What should be your immediate response in this situation?

    a. Report the violations to the appropriate authorities.

    b. Allow the offender to continue their activities without intervention.

    c. Conduct a thorough search of the offender's belongings.

    d. Issue a formal warning to the offender.

9. Scenario: Inmate Experiencing Seizure
Situation: While interacting with inmates, you notice an individual experiencing a seizure on the floor.
Question: What should be your immediate response in this situation?

    a. Call for emergency medical services (EMS) immediately

    b. Call for emergency medical services (EMS) immediately.

    c. Apply some basic first aid - getting the inmate comfortable, removing obstacles.

    d. Attempt to physically restrain the inmate to prevent injury.

10. Scenario: Response to Fire Situation:
Situation: While on duty, you discover a small fire in an inmate's cell, and smoke is starting to fill the area.
Question: What should be your immediate response in this situation?

    a. Evacuate nearby inmates and secure the area to prevent further spread.

    b. Activate the facility's fire alarm system and call for backup

    c. Ignore the fire and continue regular duties.

    d. Attempt to extinguish the fire using the nearest fire extinguisher.

11. Scenario: Response to Environmental Hazard
Situation: You receive a report of a hazardous chemical spill in the facility's storage area, and there is a strong odor in the vicinity.
Question: What should be your immediate response in this situation?

>a. Investigate the spill and attempt to clean it up on your own.
>
>b. Secure the area, isolate the spill, and evacuate nearby individuals.
>
>c. Ignore the report unless the odor becomes more severe.
>
>d. Call for assistance but continue regular duties.

12. Scenario: Response to Medical Emergency
Situation: While conducting rounds, you find an inmate who is unconscious and not breathing.
Question: What should be your immediate response in this situation?

>a. Inform the supervisor but continue with your rounds.
>
>b. Initiate cardiopulmonary resuscitation (CPR) on your own.
>
>c. Ignore the situation and move on to the next area.
>
>d. Call for emergency medical services (EMS) immediately.

13. Scenario: Inmate Experiencing Chest Pain
Situation: While conducting rounds, you come across an inmate who is clutching their chest and appears to be in significant pain.
Question: What should be your immediate response in this situation?

   a. Inform the inmate to wait and seek medical attention later.

   b. Call for emergency medical services (EMS) immediately.

   c. Apply some very basic first aid - make the inmate comfortable and loosen clothing.

   d. Take the inmate to the infirmary yourself.

14. Scenario: You are new to a large institution that uses software for supervision. Trying to cheat the software is a very serious crime that failing to report a colleague that cheats the system can land you in trouble. You discover 3 colleagues trying to cheat the system.
Question: What should you do?

   a. Wait to see if they are good employees. Report them if they are lazy.

   b. Immediately report the three colleagues.

   c. Report them if they are absent on Friday.

   d. Look the other way as you have no evidence.

15. Scenario: Inmates are randomly shouting requests and you are overwhelmed.
Question: What should you do?

    a. Calmly assert order, asking inmates to voice their requests one at a time, then address each request according to its urgency and importance.

    b. Ignore the requests and walk away to avoid further stress.

    c. Immediately call for backup because you're feeling overwhelmed.

    d. Start shouting back at the inmates to regain control.

16. Scenario: As a correctional officer, you are approached by an inmate who appreciates your work and wants to offer you a job in their company upon their release.
Question: What should be your course of action?

    a. Ignore the inmate's offer and continue with your duties.

    b. Refuse the offer directly and report the interaction to your supervisor.

    c. Ask for more details about the job offer and consider it

    d. Accept the job offer immediately as it seems like a good opportunity.

Corrections Situation Judgement

17. Scenario: As a correctional officer, an inmate has made a remark suggesting that you're not fit for the job.
Question: How should you respond?

    a. Maintain professionalism, calmly acknowledging the comment and continuing to perform your duties.

    b. Ignore the comment entirely, showing no reaction to the inmate.

    c. Try to prove the inmate to prove them wrong.

    d. Respond aggressively, defending your capability and fitness for the role.

18. Scenario: An inmate consistently calls on you for minor issues, potentially wasting your time when you're busy.
Question: How should you handle this situation?

    a. Report the inmate's behavior to your supervisor, recommending that the inmate be punished.

    b. Politely reprimand the inmate for constantly bothering you.

    c. Ignore the inmate's calls and focus on your other tasks.

    d. Communicate with the inmate, explaining that you will address serious concerns but need to balance your time to attend to other duties.

19. Scenario: Inmate with Difficulty Breathing
Situation: While on duty, an inmate approaches you complaining of difficulty breathing and appears to be wheezing.
Question: What should be your immediate response in this situation?

    a. Apply CPR

    b. Apply very basic first aid - loosen clothing etc.

    c. Inform the inmate to wait and seek medical attention later.

    d. Call for emergency medical services (EMS) immediately.

20. Scenario: Unauthorized Individual in Visitor Area
Situation: While monitoring the visitor area, you notice an individual who does not have proper identification attempting to enter.
Question: What should be your immediate response in this situation?

    a. Confront the individual and demand identification.

    b. Deny entry and inform the appropriate authorities.

    c. Ignore the situation and continue with your duties.

    d. Politely ask what they are doing there.

21. Scenario: Suspicious Package in Visitor Area
Situation: During routine inspections, you discover a suspicious package in the visitor area.
Question: What should be your immediate response in this situation?

    a. Disregard the package and continue with your inspection.

    b. Radio for assistance.

    c. Open the package to investigate its contents.

    d. Evacuate the area and inform the appropriate authorities.

22. Scenario: Aggressive Visitor in the Lobby
Situation: While in the lobby, a visitor becomes verbally aggressive and starts causing a disturbance.
Question: What should be your immediate response in this situation?

    a. Confront the individual and ask they quiet down.

    b. Ignore the situation and hope it resolves on its own.

    c. Attempt to physically restrain the visitor and calm them down.

    d. Call for backup and request assistance from fellow officers.

23. Scenario: As a correctional officer, if you notice an individual attempting to gain unauthorized access to the building, and after confronting them, the situation begins to escalate.
Question: What should be your response?

    a. Allow the individual to enter to avoid a confrontation.

    b. Engage in a physical altercation with the individual to stop them from entering.

    c. Leave the individual and call for backup.

    d. Attempt to de-escalate the situation verbally while maintaining a safe distance and notifying the relevant authority or backup.

24. Scenario: Tracking Offender Compliance
Situation: One offender consistently fails to attend mandatory counseling sessions. You have documented the non-compliance and report it to the supervisor. The inmate is still not attending the counseling sessions.
Question: What should you do?

    a. Ignore the situation, as it's the responsibility of the supervisor now.

    b. Notify the supervisor of the continued non-compliance.

    c. Engage the offender in a conversation to understand their reasons for non-compliance and propose potential solutions while notifying the supervisor.

    d. Request a transfer to avoid dealing with the non-compliant offender.

25. Scenario: An inmate falsely accuses you and you feel resentment towards him. The two of you get into an extended conflict and antagonistic relationship.
Question: How should you handle this situation

a. Attempt to mediate the dispute yourself with the inmate.

b. Seek revenge and retaliate against the inmate.

c. Ignore the conflict and continue working without addressing the issue.

d. Report the situation to the appropriate authorities and request mediation or intervention.

26. Scenario: You are on shift and performing your normal duties, when a very urgent situation develops. The issue is extremely demanding and you have not handled this type of situation before.
Question: How should you handle this situation?

a. Immediately seek guidance from a more experienced colleague or supervisor and follow their instructions.

b. Ignore the situation and continue with your normal duties, hoping it will resolve on its own.

c. Panic and become overwhelmed, leading to a delay in taking any action or seeking assistance.

d. Take a moment to assess the situation, gather relevant information, and make an informed decision based on your training and knowledge.

27. Scenario: You are receiving a lot of criticism from inmates.
Question: How should you handle the situation?

    a. Ignore the criticism and avoid any interaction or engagement with the inmates, hoping the issue will resolve on its own.

    b. Retaliate and respond aggressively towards the inmates, using disrespectful language or behavior.

    c. Remain calm and professional, actively listen to the inmates' concerns, and seek opportunities for constructive dialogue and resolution.

    d. Respond non-defensively and engage with the inmates, trying to see their point of view.

28. Scenario: While conducting rounds, you witness an inmate engaging in a physical altercation with another inmate.
Question: How should you handle this situation?

    a. Ignore the altercation and continue with your rounds, assuming it will resolve on its own.

    b. Immediately call for backup and follow established protocols to intervene and separate the inmates safely.

    c. Join the altercation and use force to break up the fight.

    d. Try to verbally intervene and de-escalate the situation without calling for backup.

29. Scenario: An inmate requests access to a restricted area without proper authorization.
Question: How should you handle this situation?

a. Provide the inmate with access to the restricted area but inform them that it is their responsibility to obtain proper authorization later.

b. Deny the request without explanation.

c. Deny the inmate's request and explain the proper authorization process to access the restricted area.

d. Allow the inmate access to the restricted area without any questioning or verification.

30. Scenario: An inmate approaches you with a complaint regarding their living conditions.
Question: How should you handle this situation?

a. React defensively, accuse the inmate of exaggerating, and refuse to address their concerns.

b. Dismiss the inmate's complaint and suggest they speak with another staff member.

c. Refer them to the proper documents.

d. Listen attentively to the inmate's complaint, empathize, and document the concern to initiate appropriate action.

31. Scenario: While transporting inmates, you encounter heavy traffic and realize you will be delayed in reaching the destination.
Question: How should you handle this situation?

a. Communicate with the appropriate authorities to inform them about the delay and follow established protocols to ensure the safety and well-being of the inmates.

b. Drive at very high speed to make up for the lost time and reach the destination as quickly as possible.

c. Ignore the delay, since it is relatively small and drive at increased speed to catch up on lost time.

d. Pull over and attempt to find alternative transportation.

32. Scenario: You notice that the seat belts in the transport vehicle are not functioning properly.
Question: How should you handle this situation?

a. Immediately report the issue to the appropriate authorities and refuse to transport inmates until the seat belts are fixed or an alternative vehicle is provided.

b. Inform the inmates that seat belts are not necessary and encourage them to disregard safety precautions.

c. Continue the transport without addressing the seat belt issue, assuming it will not pose a significant risk.

d. Proceed with the transport, advising the inmates to be cautious and hold onto something while in the vehicle.

33. Scenario: A group of inmates becomes unruly and starts creating a disturbance during transport.
Question: How should you handle this situation?
Ignore the disturbance and hope that it resolves on its own.

a. Follow established protocols to de-escalate the situation, maintain control, and ensure the safety of all individuals involved.

b. Respond forcefully to regain control and silence the unruly inmates.

c. Abandon the transport vehicle and leave the inmates unattended.

d. Ignore the disturbance and hope that it resolves on its own.

34. Scenario: One of the inmates becomes ill and displays symptoms of a medical emergency during transport.
Question: How should you handle this situation?

   a. Ignore the situation until you reach the destination.

   b. Administer basic first aid and radio for assistance.

   c. Immediately call for emergency medical assistance and follow proper procedures to provide immediate aid and support to the inmate.

   d. Inform the inmate to endure the discomfort until reaching the destination where medical assistance is available.

35. Scenario: While conducting a routine cell inspection, you discover that an inmate has concealed a weapon in their cell.
Question: How should you handle this situation?

   a. Point out that the weapon is prohibited and ask for it

   b. Ignore the weapon and continue with the cell inspection, assuming it poses no immediate threat.

   c. Leave the area without taking any action or reporting the weapon.

   d. Immediately secure the area, follow established protocols, and notify the appropriate authorities to ensure the safety of all inmates and staff.

36. Scenario: A group of inmates is involved in a physical altercation in a common area of the facility.
Question: How should you handle this situation?

   a. Encourage other inmates to join the altercation or instigate further conflict.

   b. Attempt to break up the fight alone without notifying anyone, thinking it's best to handle it independently.

   c. Immediately call for backup, ensure the safety of all individuals, and follow established protocols to intervene and de-escalate the situation.

   d. Keeping a safe distance attempt to establish order verbally.

37. Scenario: An inmate has been demonstrating increasingly aggressive behavior towards both staff and fellow inmates.
Question: How should you handle this situation?

a. Report the behavior to the appropriate authorities, document incidents, and collaborate with the mental health team to address the underlying issues.

b. Mimic the inmate's aggressive behavior as a means of establishing authority.

c. Engage in confrontations with the inmate, attempting to control their behavior through force or intimidation.

d. Speak with the inmate about their behavior.

38. Scenario: An inmate is exhibiting signs of distress and appears to be experiencing a medical emergency.
Question: How should you handle this situation?

a. Perform basic first aid first and when you are satisfied, call for medical assistance.

b. Delay seeking medical assistance and fail to provide any aid or support.

c. Attempt to provide medical treatment beyond your training and expertise.

d. Immediately call for medical assistance, provide initial aid if trained to do so, and maintain constant communication with medical professionals until help arrives.

39. Scenario: During a routine head count, you notice that one inmate is missing from their assigned location.
Question: How should you handle this situation?

    a. Assume they will turn up on their own shortly.

    b. Do a quick search for the inmate before notifying anyone.

    c. Immediately report the missing inmate to the appropriate authorities, initiate a facility-wide search, and activate established protocols to ensure the inmate's safety and locate their whereabouts.

    d. Assume the inmate is temporarily elsewhere within the facility and proceed with the head count, neglecting to report the discrepancy.

40. Scenario: While conducting a routine search of an inmate's cell, you discover unauthorized contraband hidden in their personal belongings.
Question: How should you handle this situation?

    a. Confiscate the contraband and give a warning this time.

    b. Ignore the unauthorized contraband and proceed with the search, assuming it poses no immediate threat.

    c. Follow established protocols, confiscate the contraband, document the incident thoroughly, and report it to the appropriate authorities for further investigation and disciplinary action.

    d. Decide to keep the discovery confidential and not take any action, believing it will not impact institutional safety.

Corrections Situation Judgement

Answer Key

1. A
Confronting the individual and asking for identification is the best choice.

2. B
This ensures the safety and security of staff, inmates, and the institution. It allows for the prompt implementation of the appropriate security measures. It demonstrates adherence to emergency protocols and procedures. It minimizes the risk of further harm and maintains control in the situation.

3. C
Document the non-compliance and report it to the supervisor. This ensures that the non-compliance is properly documented for further action. It allows supervisors and relevant personnel to address the issue appropriately.
It demonstrates the commitment to offender accountability and program integrity. It minimizes the risk of non-compliance becoming a recurring issue. This the best choice
- another option, giving a verbal warning is something that should have come before - the scenario says they 'consistently' fail.

4. C
This ensures safety and allows the appropriate authorities to assess and handle the situation.

5. A
This ensures the safety of staff, inmates, and other visitors by involving backup.

6. B
This ensures that the rule violation is properly addressed and documented. It upholds the principles of offender accountability and facility safety. It allows the appropriate authorities to take necessary disciplinary measures.
It minimizes the risk of further rule violations by setting a precedent.

7. D
This reinforces positive behavior and motivates the offender to continue. It acknowledges the efforts of the offender in their rehabilitation journey. It encourages a positive and supportive environment within the facility. It promotes a sense of accountability and recognition for positive behavior.

8. A
This ensures that the violations are properly documented and addressed. It allows the appropriate authorities to take necessary disciplinary measures. It upholds the principles of offender accountability and facility security. It minimizes the risk of further contraband activities by taking action.

9. A
In a medical emergency always call for professional help first.

10. B
This response prioritizes the safety of staff, inmates, and the facility. Activating the fire alarm system alerts others, allowing for a coordinated response to the fire. Calling for backup ensures additional personnel trained in fire response are on their way. Prompt action is crucial to prevent the fire from spreading and minimize harm to individuals and the facility.

11. B
This response secures the area, isolating the spill, and evacuating nearby individuals. This response prioritizes the safety of staff, inmates, and the environment by containing the hazard and removing people from potential harm.

12. D
This response involves calling for emergency medical services (EMS) immediately. This ensures that trained medical professionals are notified and can provide appropriate care to the unconscious inmate.

13. B
Calling for medical help from professionals is the best option. Next applying some very simple first aid like making the inmate comfortable.

14. B
It is the right thing to do. Failing to report
might also land you in trouble. The other options, if they are
lazy or if they are absent is irrelevant.

15. A
Calmly assert order, asking inmates to voice their requests
one at a time, then address each request according to its
urgency and importance.

16. B
It is generally considered inappropriate and/or illegal as
well as unprofessional for correctional officers to engage
in personal or business relationships with inmates due to
potential conflicts of interest and ethical concerns. Refusing the offer and reporting the interaction to your supervisor
ensures transparency and preserves the professional boundaries necessary in correctional environments.

17. A
In a correctional setting, maintaining professionalism is
paramount. It's important to remain calm and composed
even when faced with provocation. Reacting aggressively or
getting into an argument can escalate the situation and is
unprofessional. Ignoring the comment entirely may seem like
a viable option, but it could potentially lead to further disrespect or disregard from inmates. Calmly acknowledging the
comment while continuing to perform your duties displays
self-control, professionalism, and emotional intelligence

18. D
As a correctional officer, it's crucial to maintain open lines
of communication and handle all inmate concerns appropriately. However, it's also essential to manage your time efficiently. By having a calm and respectful conversation with
the inmate, you can explain your position, set boundaries,
and encourage them to discern between minor issues and
significant concerns.

19. D
Call for professional medical help first. Applying CPR is not
really effective, but ignoring the problem is very ineffective.

20. D
The first and best option is non confrontational. If that doesn't work there is lots of room to move forward with a more aggressive approach.

21. B
The best response is getting assistance, then evacuating. The worst response is opening or disregarding.

22. A
The first and best option is to confront in a non-confrontational way and then you can escalate your response if necessary.

23. D
It is important to ensure your own safety and the safety of others while dealing with potentially dangerous situations. Attempting to de-escalate the situation verbally while keeping a safe distance and calling for backup ensures that the officer maintains control over the situation without putting themselves or others at unnecessary risk.

24. C
Engaging in a conversation as well as notifying the supervisor is the best response.

25. D
By reporting the situation to the appropriate authorities and requesting mediation or intervention, you take proactive steps to address the conflict and seek a resolution. Seeking revenge or retaliating against the inmate (option A) only escalates the situation and is not a productive or professional approach.

26. A
In a high-pressure and unfamiliar situation, seeking guidance from a more experienced colleague or supervisor is the most effective response. This allows you to tap into their expertise and benefit from their knowledge to handle the urgent situation appropriately. It demonstrates your ability to recognize your limitations and seek support, which helps ensure a safe and effective resolution. Assessing the situation is an effective response where you assess and make an

informed decision based on your training and knowledge. Panicking and becoming overwhelmed can hinder your ability to take prompt and appropriate action. Ignoring the situation and hoping it will resolve on its own can lead to negative consequences and potentially jeopardize the safety and security of the environment.

27. C
In the scenario where you are receiving a lot of criticism from inmates, the most effective response (option A) is to remain calm and professional, actively listen to the inmates' concerns, and seek opportunities for constructive dialogue and resolution. This approach shows respect for the inmates' perspectives and allows for meaningful engagement to address their concerns. It demonstrates professionalism and the ability to manage difficult situations while maintaining a positive working environment.

28. B
In a situation involving a physical altercation between inmates, it is crucial to prioritize safety and follow established protocols. Calling for backup ensures assistance is on the way and helps maintain control over the situation. Attempting to verbally intervene may not be effective in halting the altercation, potentially putting yourself and others at risk. Ignoring the situation can lead to further escalation and compromise the safety and security of the facility. Joining the altercation and using force is highly inappropriate and can result in harm to yourself, other inmates, or staff members.

29. C
To ensure security and adherence to protocols, it is essential to deny unauthorized access requests from inmates. Denying the inmate's request and explaining the proper authorization process maintains the integrity of restricted areas and emphasizes the importance of following the appropriate procedures.

30. D
When an inmate approaches with a complaint, it is essential to show professionalism, attentiveness, and empathy. Actively listening to the inmate's complaint, empathizing, and documenting the concern demonstrate respect for their perspective and a commitment to addressing their issues.

31. A
In a situation where you encounter heavy traffic during inmate transport, it is crucial to prioritize the safety of the inmates and adhere to established protocols. Communicating with the appropriate authorities allows them to be informed about the delay and make any necessary adjustments or arrangements.

32. A
The safety of inmates during transport is of utmost importance, and any malfunctioning safety equipment should be addressed promptly. Reporting the issue to the appropriate authorities ensures that the problem is recognized and appropriate actions are taken to rectify it.

33. A
In a situation where inmates become unruly and create a disturbance during transport, maintaining control and ensuring the safety of all individuals involved is paramount. Following established protocols to de-escalate the situation (option A) demonstrates professionalism and a commitment to the well-being of both staff and inmates. Responding forcefully could be a good response but could easily escalate the situation and increase the risk of harm to everyone involved.

34. C
In a situation where an inmate displays symptoms of a medical emergency during transport, it is essential to prioritize their health and well-being. Immediately calling for emergency medical assistance ensures that the inmate receives timely and appropriate care.

35. D
Discovering a concealed weapon in an inmate's cell poses a significant threat to the safety and security of the institution. It is crucial to prioritize the safety of all individuals involved. Immediately securing the area, following established protocols, and notifying the appropriate authorities allows for a coordinated response to mitigate the risk and ensure the safety of both inmates and staff.

36. C
A physical altercation among inmates poses a significant risk to safety and security within the facility. Prioritizing the safety of all individuals involved is paramount. Immediately calling for backup, ensuring safety, and following established protocols allows for a coordinated and controlled response to intervene and de-escalate the situation.

37. A
Recognizing and addressing increasingly aggressive behavior is crucial to maintaining a safe and secure environment. Reporting the behavior to the appropriate authorities, documenting incidents, and collaborating with the mental health team ensures a comprehensive approach to address the underlying issues.

38. D
Responding to an inmate exhibiting signs of distress and a potential medical emergency requires prompt and appropriate action. Immediately calling for medical assistance, providing initial aid within your training and capabilities, and maintaining constant communication with medical professionals (option A) ensures the inmate receives timely and necessary care.

39. C
Noticing a missing inmate during a routine head count is a critical situation that requires immediate attention. Prioritizing inmate accountability and safety is of utmost importance. Reporting the missing inmate to the appropriate authorities, initiating a facility-wide search, and activating established protocols allows for a swift and coordinated response to locate the inmate, ensuring their well-being and maintaining institutional security.

40. C
Discovering unauthorized contraband during a routine cell search is a serious matter that must be addressed promptly and appropriately. Following established protocols, confiscating the contraband, documenting the incident thoroughly, and reporting it to the appropriate authorities (option A) ensures the integrity of institutional security, promotes inmate accountability, and facilitates further investigation and disciplinary action.

Quiz 2

Test Overview:

This assessment presents a series of hypothetical, work-related scenarios. Each scenario is followed by possible responses. Your task is to evaluate these responses based on their effectiveness in addressing the given situation.

Response Selection:

For each scenario, you will be asked to:

Select the Most Effective Response: Choose the option you believe best resolves or manages the situation.

Answering Guidelines:

- Base your judgments on the information provided in each scenario.
- Consider best practices, ethical standards, and professional behavior relevant to the role.
- There are no "trick" questions; focus on practical and appropriate actions.
- Read each scenario and its corresponding responses carefully before making selections.
- Ensure you understand the context and nuances of each situation.

Quiz 2

Answer Sheet

	A	B	C	D	E		A	B	C	D	E
1	○	○	○	○	○	21	○	○	○	○	○
2	○	○	○	○	○	22	○	○	○	○	○
3	○	○	○	○	○	23	○	○	○	○	○
4	○	○	○	○	○	24	○	○	○	○	○
5	○	○	○	○	○	25	○	○	○	○	○
6	○	○	○	○	○	26	○	○	○	○	○
7	○	○	○	○	○	27	○	○	○	○	○
8	○	○	○	○	○	28	○	○	○	○	○
9	○	○	○	○	○	29	○	○	○	○	○
10	○	○	○	○	○	30	○	○	○	○	○
11	○	○	○	○	○	31	○	○	○	○	○
12	○	○	○	○	○	32	○	○	○	○	○
13	○	○	○	○	○						
14	○	○	○	○	○						
15	○	○	○	○	○						
16	○	○	○	○	○						
17	○	○	○	○	○						
18	○	○	○	○	○						
19	○	○	○	○	○						
20	○	○	○	○	○						

Corrections Situation Judgement

1. During a fire emergency in the corrections facility, what should be the first action of a corrections officer?

    a. Evacuate all inmates immediately

    b. Assess the situation and activate the fire alarm

    c. Attempt to extinguish the fire using available equipment

    d. Inform the security team

2. When encountering environmental hazards such as a chemical spill, what should a corrections officer do?

    a. Contain the spill using available materials

    b. Call for professional help immediately

    c. Attempt to clean up the spill independently

    d. Ignore the hazard and continue with regular duties

3. What is the proper procedure for a corrections officer when an inmate requires immediate medical attention?

    a. Provide first aid if trained to do so

    b. Wait for medical personnel to arrive

    c. Inform the inmate to wait until the next scheduled medical check-up

    d. Ignore the inmate's requests

4. How should a corrections officer respond if an inmate complains of feeling unwell due to an unknown cause?

a. Ask the inmate to tough it out until the next meal Inform the medical staff immediately

b. Offer the inmate over-the-counter medication

c. Ignore the complaint

5. What is the appropriate action for a corrections officer witnessing a fellow officer violating safety protocols during a medical emergency?

a. Confront the officer immediately

b. Report the incident to the supervisor afterward

c. Do nothing to avoid conflict

d. Join the officer in violating safety protocols

6. When an inmate attempts to smuggle contraband into the facility, what should be the immediate response of a corrections officer?

a. Ignore the situation and let the inmate proceed with the contraband.

b. Report the incident to the supervisor and confiscate the contraband.

c. Assist the inmate in hiding the contraband.

d. Participate in the smuggling process.

7. If a visitor exhibits suspicious behavior during a routine visit to the facility, what should a corrections officer do?

    a. Ignore the behavior and continue with the visit.

    b. Politely ask the visitor to leave without further investigation.

    c. Notify the appropriate authorities or supervisor about the behavior.

    d. Engage in casual conversation to distract the visitor.

8. During a routine cell search, a corrections officer finds unauthorized items hidden by an inmate. What is the appropriate action to take?

    a. Ignore the items and leave the cell as is.

    b. Confiscate the items, document the findings, and inform the supervisor.

    c. Inform the inmate about the findings and allow them to keep the items.

    d. Assist the inmate in concealing the items better.

9. If a fellow corrections officer is observed engaging in inappropriate conduct with an inmate, what should be the immediate course of action?

    a. Confront the officer privately and warn them to stop the behavior.

    b. Report the incident to higher authorities or supervisors immediately.

    c. Stay silent and ignore the situation to avoid conflict.

    d. Join in the inappropriate conduct to avoid suspicion.

10. When faced with a potential security breach that could endanger the lives of inmates and staff, what should a corrections officer prioritize?

   a. Protecting their own safety first before addressing the breach.

   b. Ignoring the breach to prevent escalation of the situation.

   c. Ensuring the safety and security of all individuals within the facility.

   d. Alerting the media before taking action.

11. Inmate Tony is consistently late for scheduled programs. As a corrections officer, what is the most appropriate action to take?

   a. Confront Tony in front of other inmates to show authority

   b. Report Tony's behavior to the supervisor

   c. Ignore Tony's tardiness

   d. Assign Tony extra duties as punishment

12. What should a corrections officer do if an inmate refuses to comply with a security procedure?

   a. Issue a warning

   b. Use physical force

   c. Seek assistance from supervisor

   d. Ignore the refusal

13. In the event of a security breach, what is the primary responsibility of a corrections officer?

    a. Notify authorities

    b. Secure the area

    c. Restrain the inmates

    d. Conduct a search

14. During a group therapy session, an inmate becomes disruptive and starts arguing with others. How should the corrections officer handle this situation?

    a. Physically restrain the inmate immediately

    b. Ask the other inmates to leave the room

    c. Engage in a calm conversation to de-escalate the situation

    d. Ignore the disruptive behavior

15. An inmate requests to speak with you privately about a personal matter. What is the appropriate course of action?

    a. Deny the request as it violates rules of privacy

    b. Listen to the inmate but refrain from offering any advice

    c. Inform the inmate that all conversations are monitored

    d. Grant the request and have a private conversation in a designated area

16. **An inmate accuses another inmate of stealing his belongings. How should the corrections officer approach this situation?**

   a. Punish both inmates to set an example

   b. Ignore the accusation as it may be false

   c. Conduct a thorough investigation to gather evidence

   d. Ask both inmates to solve the issue independently

17. **A visitor attempts to bring in a prohibited item during a security check. What should the corrections officer do?**

   a. Allow the visitor to keep the item and enter the facility

   b. Confiscate the item and allow the visitor in

   c. Deny entry to the visitor and inform the supervisor

   d. Ignore the situation and let the visitor pass

18. **A conflict arises between two inmates in the facility. How should the corrections officer handle the situation?**

   a. Let the inmates resolve the conflict on their own

   b. Intervene immediately to de-escalate the situation

   c. Ignore the conflict and walk away

   d. Report the incident after the conflict has escalated

Corrections Situation Judgement

19. An inmate requests special privileges in exchange for information on illegal activities within the facility. How should the corrections officer respond?

    s. Agree to the inmate's request to obtain the information

    b. Report the inmate's offer to higher authorities

    c. Keep the information confidential and grant the privileges

    d. Ignore the inmate's request and continue regular duties

20. During a perimeter patrol, a corrections officer notices a breach in the fencing. What is the immediate action to take?

    a. Ignore the breach and continue the patrol

    b. Secure the area and call for backup

    c. Wait until the end of the shift to report the breach

    d. Inform other officers but take no action

21. What is the first step when dealing with a potentially non-compliant inmate?

    a. Remain calm and assess the situation

    b. Call for backup immediately

    c. Issue a warning to the inmate

    d. Physically restrain the inmate

22. When documenting an incident involving an inmate, what information should be included?

    a. Only factual details without opinions

    b. Opinions and personal biases

    c. Information that supports the inmate's perspective

    d. Complete and accurate details of the incident

23. During a routine cell search, what must a corrections officer prioritize?

   a. Inmate's privacy rights

   b. Speed of the search process

   c. Safety of all individuals involved

   d. Finding contraband at any cost

24. How should a corrections officer respond to an inmate who is making threats against others?

   a. Ignore the threats unless they become physical

   b. Report the threats to the supervisor immediately

   c. Confront the inmate directly about the threats

   d. Make a note of the threats for future reference

25. What is the importance of maintaining regular communication with inmates?

   a. It helps build positive relationships

   b. It increases the likelihood of escape attempts

   c. It is not necessary for corrections officers

   d. It can lead to favoritism towards certain inmates

26. An inmate is threatening another inmate with physical harm. What is the most appropriate course of action for the corrections officer?

   a. Confront the threatening inmate in front of others

   b. Separate the two inmates and de-escalate the situation

   c. Ignore the situation and let them resolve it themselves

   d. Report the incident to the supervisor immediately

Corrections Situation Judgement

27. A group of inmates is engaging in disruptive behavior during mealtime. What should the corrections officer do first?

    a. Physically restrain the disruptive inmates

    b. Verbally reprimand the entire group

    c. Inform the inmates of the consequences of their behavior

    d. Seek assistance from other staff members

28. A new inmate is exhibiting signs of distress and isolation. How can the corrections officer best address this situation?

    a. Avoid interacting with the inmate to respect their privacy

    b. Initiate a conversation with the inmate and offer support or counseling resources

    c. Assign the inmate to solitary confinement to prevent any disturbances

    d. Request the inmate's family to intervene and provide emotional support

29. What should corrections officers do if there is an unexpected delay during inmate transportation?

    a. Continue without informing anyone

    b. Inform the authorities immediately

    c. Ask the inmates to get off the vehicle

    d. Take a different route

30. What is the recommended practice for restraints when transporting inmates by vehicle?

    a. No restraints needed

    b. Loosely applied restraints

    c. Properly secured restraints

    d. Handcuffs only

31. Why is it essential to have a backup communication system during inmate transportation?

    a. To play music

    b. In case the main system fails

    c. To make announcements

    d. To communicate with other vehicles

32. What role does planning play in ensuring the security of inmates during transportation?

    a. No role

    b. Minor role

    c. Supportive role

    d. Critical role

Answer Key

1. B
The best response is to assess the situation and activate the fire alarm first because ensuring the safety of all individuals in the facility is the top priority before taking further action.

2. B
The best response is calling for professional help is also important.

3. A
It is important for corrections officers to provide first aid if trained to do so in order to address the immediate medical needs of the inmate. Delaying medical assistance can lead to serious consequences.

4. B
The best response is to inform the medical staff immediately because the inmate's condition may be serious and necessitate timely medical evaluation and treatment.

5. B
The correct action is to report the incident to the supervisor afterward to ensure accountability and address any breaches in safety protocols without escalating the situation during the emergency.

6. B
The best response is B. Reporting the incident to the supervisor and confiscating the contraband is crucial for maintaining the security of the institution and preventing potential harm to other inmates and staff.

7. C
The best response is C. Notifying the appropriate authorities or supervisor about the suspicious behavior is essential to address any potential security threats and protect the safety of the institution and the public.

8. B
The best response is B. Confiscating the unauthorized items, documenting the findings, and informing the supervisor are necessary steps to ensure the safety and security of the facility, preventing further rule violations.

9. B
The best response is B. Reporting the misconduct to higher authorities or supervisors is crucial to maintain the integrity of the corrections institution, uphold professional standards, and protect the welfare of inmates.

10. C
The best response is C. Ensuring the safety and security of all individuals within the facility should be the top priority for a corrections officer in handling any security breach to prevent harm and maintain order.

11. B
Reporting Tony's behavior to the supervisor is the correct action as it maintains professionalism, follows protocol, and ensures that appropriate measures can be taken to address the issue effectively.

12. C
The best response is 'Seek assistance from supervisor.' In cases where an inmate refuses to comply, seeking assistance from a supervisor is necessary to handle the situation professionally and ensure security measures are followed.

13. B
The best response is 'Secure the area.' The primary responsibility of a corrections officer during a security breach is to secure the area to prevent further escalation and ensure the safety of staff and inmates.

14. C
Engaging in a calm conversation to de-escalate the situation is the most effective approach as it can help diffuse tension, promote communication, and prevent further escalation among the inmates.

Corrections Situation Judgement

15. D
Granting the request and having a private conversation in a designated area is crucial for building trust with the inmate, showing empathy, and addressing any personal issues discreetly while maintaining a professional boundary.

16. C
Conducting a thorough investigation to gather evidence is essential to determine the truth, ensure fairness, and take appropriate actions based on factual information rather than assumptions or bias.

17. C
The best response is to deny entry to the visitor and inform the supervisor. Security of the institution and public safety are top priorities, and any breach of security should be addressed promptly by following proper protocols.

18. B
The best response is to intervene immediately to de-escalate the situation. As a corrections officer, maintaining control and preventing any violence within the institution is crucial for the safety of both inmates and staff.

19. B
The best response is to report the inmate's offer to higher authorities. Upholding ethical standards and following proper procedures is crucial in maintaining a secure and fair correctional environment.

20. B
The best response is to secure the area and call for backup. Any breach in the perimeter poses a significant security risk, and immediate action is necessary to prevent any potential escape or threat to the institution and the public.

21. A
The best response is A. Remaining calm and assessing the situation allows the corrections officer to evaluate the level of risk and determine the appropriate course of action before escalating the situation.

22. D
The best response is D. Documenting complete and accurate details of the incident ensures transparency and provides an objective record for future reference and evaluation.

23. C
The best response is C. Prioritizing the safety of all individuals involved, including officers and inmates, is crucial to maintaining a secure and respectful environment during a cell search.

24. B
The best response is B. Reporting threats to the supervisor immediately allows for proper assessment and intervention, ensuring the safety of all individuals within the facility.

25. A
The best response is A. Regular communication with inmates helps build trust, manage conflicts, and promote a safer and more constructive environment within the correctional facility.

26. B
The best response is to separate the two inmates and de-escalate the situation. As a corrections officer, maintaining security is crucial, and diffusing potential violence by separating conflicting parties helps prevent harm to both inmates and staff.

27. C
The best response is to inform the inmates of the consequences of their behavior. Communicating the potential outcomes of their actions can deter further disruptions and promote order within the facility.

28. B
The best response is to initiate a conversation with the inmate and offer support or counseling resources. Building rapport and showing empathy towards distressed inmates can help alleviate their feelings of isolation and promote mental well-being within the correctional setting.

29. B
The best response is 'Inform the authorities immediately.' Communication is crucial in such situations to ensure proper protocols are followed and to maintain the security of the inmates.

30. C
The best response is 'Properly secured restraints.' Using appropriate restraints ensures the safety and security of both the inmates and officers during transportation.

31. B
The best response is 'In case the main system fails.' Having a backup communication system is crucial to maintain communication in case of any technical issues with the primary system, ensuring continuous contact and coordination during transportation.

32. D
The best response is 'Supportive role.' Planning plays a critical role in organizing and preparing for safe inmate transportation, supporting the implementation of security measures and protocols to safeguard the inmates throughout the process.

Dilemma and Judgement Analysis 1

Response to Fire in a Correctional Facility

Context

Imagine you are the head of security in a correctional facility that has just experienced a fire outbreak in one of the housing units. The incident has resulted in an immediate threat to both the safety of the inmates and the integrity of the building. You are faced with a critical decision that embodies the ontological dilemma of prioritizing the safety of individuals versus the safety of the facility itself.

Description of the Dilemma
As the head of security, you have two primary responsibilities: ensuring the safety of the inmates and protecting the physical structure of the facility. The fire is spreading rapidly, and time is of the essence.

Safety of Inmates: Your first instinct is to prioritize the evacuation of the inmates from the affected area. This is crucial because their lives are at risk due to smoke inhalation, flames, and potential structural collapse. However, many inmates are uncooperative, either due to panic or discontent with authority. Some may refuse to leave their cells without a proper head count, while others could take this as an opportunity to escape.

Safety of the Building: On the other hand, the integrity of the building must also be considered. A complete evacuation could lead to chaos and potential breaches of security, putting not only the staff but also other inmates at risk. Moreover, if the fire spreads to other areas of the facility, it could result in a much larger disaster, potentially compromising evidence and causing damage that could take months to repair.

OPTIONS

You have several options to consider:

- **Evacuate Immediately:** Direct all inmates to evacuate the building, risking some to potential escapes and security breaches.
- **Containment Strategy:** Focus on containing the fire and securing the building while attempting to manage the evacuation in a controlled manner. This may involve using lock-down procedures to prevent inmate escapes.
- **Call for External Help:** Contact local fire services and wait for their arrival before taking any action, which could result in delays but might ensure that trained professionals handle the situation.

ANALYSIS OF OPTIONS

Evacuate Immediately:
Pros: Protects lives and minimizes potential harm to inmates.
Cons: High risk of inmate escapes, potential for violence, and loss of control over the facility.

Containment Strategy:
Pros: Balances the need to save lives while maintaining control of the situation within the facility.
Cons: Risk of underestimating the fire's spread, leading to greater danger for inmates.

Call for External Help:

Pros: Leverages professional fire fighting resources equipped to handle large fires effectively.

Cons: Delays in response could exacerbate the situation, and you may lose precious time in which lives are at stake.

Conclusion: The Best Solution

After weighing the implications of each option, the best solution is to implement a Containment Strategy. While immediate evacuation seems to prioritize inmate safety, it poses significant risks of breach and chaos, which could ultimately lead to more harm than good. By establishing a controlled evacuation plan while simultaneously working to contain the fire, you can create a safer environment for both inmates and staff.

This approach allows you to prioritize the physical safety of the inmates while still being vigilant about the security of the facility. By deploying trained staff to guide inmates out in an orderly fashion and coordinating with fire services for rapid intervention, you can mitigate risks and ensure that the situation is managed effectively. The priority should remain on life preservation, but with a strategy that maintains the integrity of the correctional environment as much as possible.

Dilemma and Judgement Analysis 2

Ensuring Safety in a Corrections Institution

Scenario

In a medium-security corrections institution, tensions among inmates have escalated due to overcrowding and limited resources. Reports indicate an increase in violent incidents, gang affiliations, and overall inmate unrest. The staff is stretched thin, with several positions unfilled, leading to longer shifts and diminished morale among correctional officers. As a newly appointed warden, you face a critical decision that could significantly impact the safety of both inmates and staff.

The Dilemma

You have two primary options to address the escalating safety concerns:

- **Increase Security Measures:** Implement strict lockdown procedures, enhance surveillance through additional cameras, and increase the number of correctional officers on duty. This approach aims to deter violence and maintain order but may further aggravate tensions among inmates who feel restricted and oppressed by constant surveillance.

Focus on Rehabilitation and Support Services: Invest in programs aimed at inmate rehabilitation, such as educational opportunities, vocational training, and counseling services. This approach seeks to reduce recidivism and improve overall inmate behavior. However, it requires reallocating funds from security budgets and may lead to criticisms of being too lenient during a time of heightened violence.

Analysis of Safety Concerns

To navigate this dilemma, it is essential to consider the following safety aspects of the corrections institution:

- **Inmate Health and Welfare:** A safe facility must prioritize the physical and psychological well-being of inmates. Increased security measures may lead to mental health deterioration among inmates, particularly if they perceive the environment as oppressive.

- **Staff Morale and Retention:** High-stress environments with insufficient support can lead to burnout and high turnover rates among correctional officers. Low morale and staff shortages can exacerbate safety issues, as experienced personnel are crucial in managing conflicts and maintaining order.

- **Community Safety:** The safety of the surrounding community is also at stake. A facility that fails to rehabilitate inmates may contribute to higher recidivism rates, leading to more crime in the community after their release.

- **Public Perception and Accountability:** The public expects corrections institutions to ensure safety for all involved. Poor management in addressing safety concerns can lead to negative perceptions and decreased trust in the correctional system.

Best Solution

After thorough consideration of both options and the implications of each, the best solution is to implement a balanced approach that combines increased security measures with enhanced rehabilitation and support services.

- **Short-term Security Enhancements:** Immediately bolster security with additional staff during peak hours and implement de-escalation training for officers to manage conflicts effectively. Install more surveillance equipment to monitor high-risk areas without infringing excessively on inmate privacy.

- **Long-term Investment in Rehabilitation:** Allocate a portion of the budget towards developing and expanding rehabilitation programs. Engage community organizations to provide educational and vocational opportunities, while also addressing mental health needs.

- **Stakeholder Engagement:** Involve staff, inmates, and community leaders in discussions about safety and rehabilitation. Open communication channels can help identify issues early and foster a cooperative environment.

- **Evaluation and Adaptation:** Establish a task force to continuously evaluate the effectiveness of implemented measures. Regular assessments will allow for adjustments based on the evolving dynamics within the institution.

By balancing security with rehabilitation, the institution can create a safer environment that promotes inmate well-being while ensuring the safety of staff and the surrounding community. This holistic approach acknowledges the complexity of corrections and the necessity of addressing multiple facets to improve overall safety.

Dilemma and Judgement Analysis 3

Balancing Inmate Accountability

Scenario

You are a correctional officer in a medium-security prison, dealing with a rising number of incidents where inmates refuse to take responsibility for their actions. Recently, there have been several altercations among inmates, and reports of contraband being smuggled into the facility have increased. As part of your role, you have been tasked with implementing a new program aimed at improving inmate accountability.

The prison administration provides you with two options to choose from:

- **Strict Punitive Measures:** This option involves implementing a zero-tolerance policy towards any misconduct. Inmates found engaging in conflicts or possessing contraband would face immediate disciplinary actions, including isolation or loss of privileges. The intention is to instill fear of consequences, hoping it will deter negative behavior.

- **Restorative Justice Approach:** This option focuses on dialogue and rehabilitation. Inmates involved in misconduct would participate in restorative circles where they can discuss their actions, understand their impact on others, and work corroboratively to make amends. This approach promotes personal accountability and encourages inmates to reflect on their choices in a supportive environment.

The Dilemma

You must decide which approach to implement to improve inmate accountability. While the strict punitive measures may lead to immediate compliance and a decrease in visible incidents, they could also foster resentment, fear, and an adversarial atmosphere between staff and inmates. This might ultimately hinder long-term rehabilitation efforts. Conversely, while the restorative justice approach could cultivate a more positive environment and promote genuine reflection and accountability among inmates, it runs the risk of being perceived as lenient, potentially leading to further misconduct if not taken seriously by all inmates.

Best Solution

The recommended solution is to adopt the Restorative Justice Approach.

Explanation

The choice of the restorative justice approach aligns more closely with the ultimate goal of corrections: rehabilitation and reintegration into society. By facilitating discussions that allow inmates to acknowledge their behaviors and their effects, this method fosters a deeper understanding of accountability. It encourages personal growth and the development of empathy, which are crucial for reducing recidivism rates.

- **Promotes Understanding:** Inmates are given a platform to express their feelings and experiences, which can help them process their actions more constructively.

- **Encourages Responsibility:** Through dialogue, inmates learn to see themselves as part of a community. They begin to recognize how their actions affect not only their own lives but also the lives of others, fostering a sense of responsibility.

- Builds Relationships: Restorative practices can improve the relationship between staff and inmates. A supportive environment where accountability is emphasized rather than purely punitive can lead to better communication and trust.

Long-Term Benefits: While immediate compliance might be less evident compared to strict punitive measures, the long-term benefits of reduced recidivism and improved inmate behavior will outweigh short-term successes.

While both approaches have their merits, the restorative justice model offers a more holistic route to improving inmate accountability, addressing the identity, morality, and the potential for transformation within each individual. This model aligns with the core objectives of correctional facilities: to rehabilitate rather than punish.

Dilemma and Judgement Analysis 4

Security of Inmates

Scenario

In a medium-security correctional facility in Canada, a corrections officer named Officer Lee is faced with a challenging situation that tests her ethical beliefs and decision-making skills regarding the security of inmates.

Officer Lee has been observing a pattern of behavior among a group of inmates who have become increasingly aggressive towards one another. Recently, inmate Thompson, known for his violent past, has been seen conversing with several other inmates, and there are rumors that they may be planning an altercation. Officer Lee has a duty to maintain the safety and security of all inmates within the facility, but she also understands that it is crucial to ensure that inmates' rights are respected.

One afternoon, Officer Lee overhears Thompson discussing "settling scores" with another inmate. The conversation suggests a potential fight that could harm not only the individuals involved but also other inmates and staff members. She is aware that reporting this to her superiors could lead to preemptive disciplinary action against Thompson and his associates, potentially exacerbating tensions and leading to further violence. However, if she chooses to ignore it, she risks the safety of everyone involved.

Dilemma and Judgment Analysis

The Dilemma

Officer Lee must decide whether to:

- **Report the overheard conversation** to her superiors and take immediate action to prevent any potential violence. This approach may protect the safety of the inmates in the short term, but it could also escalate tensions and create feelings of mistrust among the inmates, particularly if they perceive her as a traitor or as someone who cannot be trusted.

- **Confront Thompson directly and attempt to mediate the situation herself.** This could help diffuse the immediate threat and build positive relationships with the inmates. However, it could put her in a dangerous position, as confronting a potentially volatile inmate might provoke an unpredictable reaction.

- **Do nothing and monitor the situation quietly,** hoping that tensions will decrease on their own. This choice avoids the immediate confrontation but leaves the possibility of violence unaddressed, risking harm to multiple individuals.

Best Approach/Solution

The best approach for Officer Lee is to report the overheard conversation to her superiors while simultaneously preparing to engage with Thompson and the other inmates in a constructive manner. This dual approach ensures that she upholds her ethical responsibility to protect the inmates and staff.

EXPLANATION

- **Safety First:** By reporting the potential threat, Officer Lee prioritizes the immediate safety of all individuals in the facility. It is her duty to act upon credible information that indicates a risk of violence.

- **Maintaining Professional Integrity:** Reporting the conversation demonstrates her commitment to professionalism and the protocols in place designed to ensure safety. It shows that she is vigilant and takes her responsibilities seriously.

- **Building Relationships:** Alongside her report, Officer Lee can request to facilitate a conflict resolution session with Thompson and the other inmates involved. This proactive engagement can help de-escalate tensions, empowering inmates to communicate their grievances constructively rather than through violence.

- **Preventative Measures:** Engaging in dialogue allows for addressing underlying issues that may lead to aggression among inmates. It fosters an environment where inmates feel heard and respected, which can mitigate future conflicts.

In conclusion, Officer Lee's dilemma illustrates the complexity faced by correctional officers in balancing the safety of inmates with respect for their rights. By reporting the potential threat while also seeking to mediate the situation, she navigates the ontological concerns of her role and responsibilities effectively, prioritizing both safety and human dignity.

Dilemma and Judgement Analysis 4

Security of Inmates During Transport

Scenario Overview

As a corrections officer, you are responsible for the transport of high-risk inmates from a correctional facility to a court appearance. The transport involves a multi-agency collaboration, including local law enforcement and court security. You are tasked with ensuring the safety of the inmates, your team, and the public while maintaining a secure environment.

On the day of transport, you notice that one of the inmates, who has a history of violent behavior and escape attempts, appears unusually agitated. You have been informed that there is a potential risk of an attempted escape during the transport, as intelligence indicates that a criminal organization may be planning an attack to facilitate the inmate's escape.

Corrections Situation Judgement

The Dilemma

You face a critical decision:

- **Prioritize Security Protocols:** Follow established procedures for transporting high-risk inmates, which include a strict escort system, using specialized transport vehicles, and coordinating with law enforcement for added security. This approach prioritizes the safety of everyone involved but might provoke the inmate further due to increased scrutiny and restrictions, potentially leading to aggressive behavior during transport.

- **Adjusting Protocols for Inmate Welfare**: Consider temporarily relaxing certain protocols to address the inmate's agitation, allowing for more comfort during transport. This could mean fewer restraints or a less intimidating presence during the transit. However, this approach raises concerns about the heightened risk of an escape attempt and the safety of your team and the public.

Considerations

The essence of the dilemma lies in the identity and responsibilities of the corrections officer. As a protector of the community, you must balance the duty to maintain public safety with the ethical treatment of inmates. This situation raises fundamental questions about the role of corrections officers:

- **What does it mean to be a corrections officer?** Is your primary responsibility to ensure security at all costs, even if it means subjecting an inmate to discomfort or fear?

- **How do you define justice and fairness?** Does relaxing certain protocols for the sake of an inmate's mental state compromise the integrity of the justice system?

- **What are the broader implications of your actions?** If the inmate escapes due to leniency, how does that affect public trust in the corrections system?

Potential Outcomes

If you choose to follow strict security protocols, you may successfully prevent any escape attempts, but you risk escalating the inmate's agitation, which could lead to violence during transport, endangering staff and other inmates. Additionally, the inmate's experience may contribute to long-term resentment towards the system, impacting rehabilitation efforts.

If you decide to adjust protocols, you might create a more manageable environment for the inmate, reducing immediate tension. However, if an escape occurs because of this leniency, the consequences could be severe, including potential harm to civilians and loss of trust in the corrections system. This outcome would not only jeopardize your career but also impact the safety of future transports.

Conclusion

In this scenario, the corrections officer is faced with a profound ontological dilemma that challenges their understanding of their role within the justice system. The decision made will reflect not only on personal ethics and responsibilities but will also weigh heavily on the broader implications for community safety and the effectiveness of the corrections system. Balancing security with humane treatment requires deep reflection on the core values guiding corrections and justice.

How to Prepare for a Test

Most students hide their heads and procrastinate when faced with preparing for an examination, hoping that somehow they will be spared the agony of taking that test, especially if it is a big one that their futures rely on. Avoiding the all-important test is what many students do best and unfortunately, they suffer the consequences because of their lack of preparation.

Test preparation requires strategy. It also requires dedication and persistence. It is the perfect training ground for anyone planning a professional life. Besides having several reliable strategies, successful students also have a clear goal and know how to accomplish it. These tried and true concepts have worked well and will make your test preparation easier.

The Study Approach.

Take responsibility for your own test preparation.

It is a common, and big mistake, to link your studying to someone else's. Study partners are great, but only if they are reliable. It is your job to be prepared for the test, even if a study partner fails you. Do not allow others to distract you from your goals.

Prioritize the time available to study.

When do you learn best, early in the day or in the dark of night? Does your mind absorb and retain information most efficiently in small blocks of time, or do you require long stretches to get the most done? It is important to figure out the best blocks of time available to you when you can be the most productive. Try to consolidate activities to allow for longer periods of study time.

Find a quiet place where you will not be disturbed.

Do not try to squeeze in quality study time in any old location. Find a quiet place with a minimum of distractions, such as the library, a park or even the laundry room. Good lighting is essential and you need to have comfortable seating and a desk surface large enough to hold your materials. It is probably not a great idea to study in your bedroom. You might be distracted by clothes on the floor, a book you have been planning to read, the telephone or something else. Besides, in the middle of studying, that bed will start to look very comfortable. Whatever you do, avoid using the bed as a place to study since you might fall asleep to avoid your work! That is the last thing that you should be doing during study time.

The exception is flashcards. By far the most productive study time is sitting down and studying and studying only. However, with flashcards you can carry them with you and make use of odd moments, like standing in line, or waiting for the bus. This isn't as productive, but it really helps and is definitely worth doing.

Determine what you need to study.

Gather together your books, your notes, your laptop and any other materials needed to focus on your study for this exam. Ensure you have everything you need so you don't waste time. Remember paper, pencils and erasers, sticky notes, bottled water and a snack. Keep your phone with you if you need it to find out essential information, but keep it turned off so others can't distract you.

Have a positive attitude.

It is essential that you approach your studies for the test with an attitude that says you will pass it. And pass it with flying colors! This is one of the most important keys to successful study strategy. Believing that you are capable actually helps you to become capable.

THE STRATEGY OF STUDYING

Make materials easy to review and access.

Consolidate materials to help keep your study area clutter free. If you have a laptop and a means of getting on line, you do not need a dictionary and thesaurus as well since those things are easily accessible via the internet. Go through written notes and consolidate those, as well. Have everything you need, but do not weigh yourself down with duplicates.

Review class notes.

Stay on top of class notes and assignments by reviewing them frequently and regularly. Re-writing notes can be a terrific study trick, as it helps lock in information. Pay special attention to any comments that have been made by the teacher. If a study guide has been made available as part of the class materials, use it! It will be a valuable tool to use for studying.

Estimate how much time you will need.

If you are concerned about the amount of time you have available it is a good idea to set up a schedule so that you do not get bogged down on one section and end without enough time left to study other things. Remember to schedule break time, and use that time for a little exercise or other stress reducing techniques.

Test yourself to determine your weaknesses.

Look online for additional assessment and evaluation tools available like practice questions for a particular subject. Once you have determined your weaknesses, you can focus on these, and just brush up on the other areas of the exam.

Mental Prep – How to Psych Yourself Up for a Test

Because tests contribute mightily to your final class grade or to whether you are accepted into a program, it is understandable taking tests is stressful for many students. Even students who know they have learned all the required material find their minds going blank as they stare at the words in the questions. You can avoid test anxiety by preparing yourself mentally. One easy way to overcome that anxiety is to prepare mentally for the test with a few simple techniques.

Do not procrastinate.

Study the material for the test when it becomes available, and continue to review the material until the test day. Waiting until the last minute and cramming, you increase your anxiety. This leads to negative self-talk, which becomes self-fulfilling. Telling yourself "I can't learn this. I am going to fail" is a pretty sure indication that you are right.

Positive self-talk.

Positive self-talk drowns out negative self-talk and increases your confidence. Whenever you begin feeling overwhelmed or anxious about the test, remind yourself that you have studied enough, you know the material and that you will pass the test. Use only positive words. Both negative and positive self-talk are really just your fantasy, so why not choose to be a winner?

Do not compare yourself to others.

Do not compare yourself to other students, or your performance to theirs. Instead, focus on your own strengths and weaknesses and prepare accordingly. Regardless of how others perform, your performance is the only one that effects your grade. Comparing yourself to others increases your anxiety and negative self-talk before the test.

Visualize.

Make a mental image of yourself taking the test. You know the answers and feel relaxed. Visualize doing well on the test and having no problems with the material. Visualizations can increase your confidence and decrease the anxiety you might otherwise feel before the test. Instead of thinking of this as a test, see it as an opportunity to demonstrate what you have learned!

Avoid negativity.

Worry is contagious and viral - once it gets started it builds on itself. Cut it off before it gets to be a problem. Even if you are relaxed and confident, being around anxious, worried classmates might cause you to start feeling anxious. Before the test, tune out the fears of classmates. Feeling anxious and worried before an exam is normal, and every student experiences those feelings at some point. However, you cannot allow these feelings to interfere with your performance. Practicing mental preparation techniques and remembering that the test is not the only measure of your academic performance will ease your anxiety and ensure that you perform at your best.

How to Take a Test

Everyone knows that taking an exam is stressful, but it does not have to be that bad! There are a few simple things that you can do to increase your score on any type of test. Take a look at these tips and consider how you can incorporate them into your study time.

Reading the Instructions

This is the most basic point, but one that, surprisingly, many students ignore and it can cost them big time! Since reading the instructions is one of the most common, and 100% preventable mistakes, we have a whole section just on reading instructions.

Pay close attention to the sample questions. Almost all standardized tests offer sample questions, paired with their correct solutions. Go through these to make sure that you understand what they mean and how they arrived at the correct answer. Do not be afraid to ask the test supervisor for help with a sample that confuses you, or instructions that you are unsure of.

Tips for Reading the Question

We could write pages and pages of tips just on reading the test questions. Here are the ones that will help you the most.

- **Think first.** Before you look at the answer, read and think about the question. It is best to try to come up with the correct answer before you look at the options given. This way, when the test-writer tries to trick you

with a close answer, you will not fall for it.
- **Make it true or false.** If a question confuses you, then look at each answer option and think of it as a "true" "false" question. Select the one that seems most likely to be "true."
- **Mark the Question.** Don't be afraid to mark up the test booklet. Unless you are specifically told not to mark in the booklet, use it to your advantage. More on this below.
- **Circle Key Words.** As you are reading the question, underline or circle key words. This helps you to focus on the most critical information needed to solve the problem. For example, if the question said, "Which of these is not a synonym for huge?" You might circle "not," "synonym" and "huge." That clears away the clutter and lets you focus on what is important.
- **Always underline these words:** all, none, always, never, most, best, true, false and except.
- **Cross out irrelevant choices.** If you find yourself confused by lengthy questions, cross out anything that you think is irrelevant, obviously wrong, or information that you think is offered to distract you. Elimination is the most valuable strategy!
- **Do not try to read between the lines.** Usually, questions are written to be straightforward, with no deep, underlying meaning. The simple answer really is often the correct answer. Do not over-analyze!

How to Take a Test - The Basics

Some tests are designed to assess your ability to quickly grab the necessary information; this type of exam makes speed a priority. Others are more concerned with your depth of knowledge, and how accurate it is. When you receive a test, look it over to determine whether the test is for speed or accuracy. If the test is for speed, like many standardized tests, your strategy is clear; answer as many questions as quickly as possible.

Watch out, though! There are a few tests that are designed to determine how fully and accurately you can answer the questions. Guessing on this type of test is a big mistake, because the teacher expects any student with an average grade to be able to complete the test in the time given. Racing through the test and making guesses that prove to be incorrect will cost you big time!

Every little bit helps.

If you are permitted calculators, or other materials, make sure you bring them, even if you do not think you will need them. Use everything at your disposal to increase your score.

Make time your friend.

Budget your time from the moment your pencil hits the page until you are finished with the exam, and stick to it! Virtually all standardized tests have a time limit for each section. The time permitted for each section will almost certainly be included in the instructions or printed at the top of the page. If for some reason it is not immediately visible, rather than wasting your time hunting for it you can use the points or percentage of the score as a proxy to make an educated guess of the time limit.

Use the allotted time for each section and then move onto the next section whether you have completed it or not. Stick with the instructions and you will be able to answer most the questions in each section.

With speed tests you may not be able to complete the entire test. Rest assured that you are not really expected to! The goal of this type of examination is to determine how quickly you can reach into your brain and access a particular piece of information, which is one way of determining how well you know it. If you know a test you are taking is a speed test, you will know the strategies to use for the best results.

Easy does it.

One smart way to tackle a test is to locate the easy questions and answer those first. This is a time-tested strategy that never fails. First, read the question and decide if you can answer it in less than a minute. If so, complete the question and go to the next one. If not, skip it for now and continue to the next question. By the time you have completed the first pass through this section of the exam, you will have answered a good number of questions. Not only does it boost your confidence, relieve anxiety and kick your memory up a notch, you will know exactly how many questions remain and can allot the rest of your time accordingly. Think of doing the easy questions first as a warm-up!

If you run out of time before you manage to tackle all the difficult questions, do not let it throw you. All that means is you have used your time in the most efficient way possible by answering as many questions correctly as you could. Missing a few points by not answering a question whose answer you do not know just means you spent that time answering one whose answer you did.

A word to the wise: Skipping questions for which you are drawing a complete blank is one thing, but we are not suggesting you skip every question you come across that you are not 100 % certain of. A good rule of thumb is to try to answer at least eight of every 10 questions the first time through.

Do not watch your watch.

At best, taking an important exam is an uncomfortable situation. If you are like most people, you might be tempted to subconsciously distract yourself from the task at hand. One of the most common ways is by becoming obsessed with your watch or the wall clock. Do not watch your watch! Take it off and place it on the top corner of your desk, far enough away that you will not be tempted to look at it every two minutes. Better still, turn the watch face away from you. That way, every time you try to sneak a peek, you will be reminded to refocus your attention to the task at hand. Give yourself permission to check your watch or the wall clock after you complete each section. If you know yourself to be a bit of a slow-poke in other aspects of life, you can check your watch a bit more often. Even so, focus on answering the questions, not on how many minutes have elapsed since you last looked at it.

Divide and conquer.

What should you do when you come across a question that is so complicated you may not even be certain what is being asked? As we have suggested, the first time through the section you are best off skipping the question. But at some point, you will need to return to it and get it under control. The best way to handle questions that leave you feeling so anxious you can hardly think is by breaking them into manageable pieces. Solving smaller bits is always easier. For complicated questions, divide them into bite-sized pieces and solve these smaller sets separately. Once you understand what the reduced sections are really saying, it will be much easier to put them together and get a handle on the bigger question.

Reason your way through the toughest questions.

If you find that a question is so dense you can't figure out how to break it into smaller pieces, there are a few strategies that might help. First, read the question again and look for hints. Can you re-word the question in one or more different ways? This may give you clues. Look for words that can function as either verbs or nouns, and try to figure out from the sentence structure which it is here. Remember that many nouns in English have several different meanings. While some of those meanings might be related, sometimes they are completely distinct. If reading the sentence one way does not make sense, consider a different definition or meaning for a key word.

The truth is, it is not always necessary to understand a question to arrive at a correct answer! A trick that successful students understand is using Strategy 5, Elimination.

Frequently, at least one answer is clearly wrong and can be crossed off the list of possible correct answers. Next, look at the remaining answers and eliminate any that are only partially true. You may still have to flat-out guess from time to time, but using the process of elimination will help you make your way to the correct answer more often than not - even when you don't know what the question means!

Do not leave early.

Use all the time allotted to you, even if you can't wait to get out of the testing room. Instead, once you have finished, spend the remaining time reviewing your answers. Go back to those questions that were most difficult for you and review your response. Another good way to use this time is to return to multiple-choice questions in which you filled in a bubble. Do a spot check, reviewing every fifth or sixth question to make sure your answer coincides with the bubble you filled in. This is a great way to catch yourself if you made a mistake, skipped a bubble and therefore put all your answers in the wrong bubbles!

Become a super sleuth and look for careless errors. Look for questions that have double negatives or other odd phrasing; they might be an attempt to throw you off. Careless errors on your part might be the result of skimming a question and missing a key word. Words such as "always," "never," "sometimes," "rarely" and the like can give a strong indication of the answer the question is really seeking. Don't throw away points by being careless!

Just as you budgeted time at the beginning of the test to allow for easy and more difficult questions, be sure to budget sufficient time to review your answers. On essay questions and math questions where you are required to show your work, check your writing to make sure it is legible.

Math questions can be especially tricky. The best way to double check math questions is by figuring the answer using a different method, if possible.

Here is another terrific tip. It is likely that no matter how hard you try, you will have a handful of questions you just are not sure of. Keep them in mind as you read through the rest of the test. If you can't answer a question, looking back over the test to find a different question that addresses the same topic might give you clues.

We know that taking the test has been stressful and you can hardly wait to escape. Just Leaving before you double-check as much as possible can be a quick trip to disaster. Taking a few extra minutes can make the difference between getting a bad grade and a great one. Besides, there will be lots of time to relax and celebrate after the test is turned in.

In the Test Room – What you MUST do!

If you are like the rest of the world, there is almost nothing you would rather avoid than taking a test. Unfortunately, that is not an option if you want to pass. Rather than suffer, consider a few attitude adjustments that might turn the experience from a horrible one to…well, an interesting one! Take a look at these tips. Simply changing how you perceive the experience can change the experience itself.

Get in the mood.

After weeks of studying, the big day has finally arrived. The worst thing you can do to yourself is arrive at the test site feeling frustrated, worried, and anxious. Keep a check on your emotional state. If your emotions are shaky before a test it can determine how well you do on the test. It is extremely important that you pump yourself up, believe in yourself, and use that confidence to get in the mood!

Don't fight reality.

Oftentimes, students resent tests, and with good reason. After all, many people do not test well, and they know the grade they end with does not accurately reflect their true knowledge. It is easy to feel resentful because tests classify students and create categories that just don't seem fair. Face it: Students who are great at rote memorization and not that good at actually analyzing material often score higher than those who might be more creative thinkers and balk at simply memorizing cold, hard facts. It may not be fair, but there it is anyway. Conformity is an asset on tests, and creativity is often a liability. There is no point in wasting time or energy being upset about this reality. Your first step is to accept the reality and get used to it. You will get higher marks when you realize tests do count and that you must give them your best effort. Think about your future and the career that is easier to achieve if you have consistently earned high grades. Avoid negative energy and focus on anything that lifts your enthusiasm and increases your motivation.

Get there early enough to relax.

If you are wound up, tense, scared, anxious, or feeling rushed, it will cost you. Get to the exam room early and relax before you go in. This way, when the exam starts, you are comfortable and ready to apply yourself. Of course, you do not want to arrive so early that you are the only one there. That will not help you relax; it will only give you too much time to sit there, worry and get wound up all over again.

If you can, visit the room where you will be taking your exam a few days ahead of time. Having a visual image of the room can be surprisingly calming, because it takes away one of the big 'unknowns'. Not only that, but once you have visited, you know how to get there and will not be worried about getting lost. Furthermore, driving to the test site once lets you know how much time you need to allow for the trip. That means three potential stressors have been eliminated all at once.

Get it down on paper.

One advantage of arriving early is that it allows you time to recreate notes. If you spend a lot of time worrying about whether you will be able to remember information like names, dates, places, and mathematical formulas, there is a solution for that. Unless the exam you are taking allows you to use your books and notes, (and very few do) you will have to rely on memory. Arriving early gives to time to tap into your memory and jot down key pieces of information you know will be asked. Just make certain you are allowed to make notes once you are in the testing site; not all locations will permit it. Once you get your test, on a small piece of paper write down everything you are afraid you will forget. It will take a minute or two but by dumping your worries onto the page you have effectively eliminated a certain amount of anxiety and driven off the panic you feel.

Get comfortable in your chair.

Here is a clever technique that releases physical stress and helps you get comfortable, even relaxed in your body. You will tense and hold each of your muscles for just a few seconds. The trick is, you must tense them hard for the technique to work. You might want to practice this technique a few times at home; you do not want an unfamiliar technique to add to your stress just before a test, after all! Once you are at the test site, this exercise can always be done in the rest room or another quiet location.

Start with the muscles in your face then work down your body. Tense, squeeze and hold the muscles for a moment or two. Notice the feel of every muscle as you go down your body. Scowl to tense your forehead, pull in your chin to tense your neck. Squeeze your shoulders down to tense your back. Pull in your stomach all the way back to your ribs, make your lower back tight then stretch your fingers. Tense your leg muscles and calves then stretch your feet and your toes. You should be as stiff as a board throughout your entire body.

Now relax your muscles in reverse starting with your toes. Notice how all the muscles feel as you relax them one by one. Once you have released a muscle or set of muscles, allow them to remain relaxed as you proceed up your body. Focus on how you are feeling as all the tension leaves. Start breathing deeply when you get to your chest muscles. By the time you have found your chair, you will be so relaxed it will feel like bliss!

Fight distraction.

A lucky few are able to focus deeply when taking an important examination, but most people are easily distracted, probably because they would rather be anyplace else! There are several things you can do to protect yourself from distraction.

Stay away from windows. If you sit near a window you are adding an unnecessary distraction.

Choose a seat away from the aisle so you do not become distracted by people who leave early. People who leave the exam room early are often the ones who fail. Do not compare your time to theirs.

Of course, you love your friends; that's why they are your friends! In the test room, however, they should become complete strangers inside your mind. Forget they are there. The first step is to physically distance yourself from friends or classmates. That way, you will not be tempted to glance at them to see how they are doing, and there will be no chance of eye contact that could either distract you or even lead to an accusation of cheating. Furthermore, if they are feeling stressed because they did not spend the focused time studying that you did, their anxiety is less likely to permeate your hard-earned calm.

Of course, you will want to choose a seat where there is sufficient light. Nothing is worse than trying to take an important examination under flickering lights or dim bulbs.

Ask the instructor or exam proctor to close the door if there is a lot of noise outside. If the instructor or proctor is unable to do so, block out the noise as best you can. Do not let anything disturb you.

Make sure you have enough pencils, pens and whatever else you will need. Many entrance exams do not permit you to bring personal items such as candy bars into the testing room. If so, be sure to eat a nutritionally balanced breakfast. Eat protein, complex carbohydrates and a little fat to keep you feeling full and to supercharge your energy. Nothing is worse than a sudden drop in blood sugar during an exam.

Do not allow yourself to become distracted by being too cold or hot. Regardless of the weather outside, carry a sweater, scarf or jacket if the air conditioning at the test site is set too high, or the heat set too low. By the same token, dress in layers so that you are prepared for a range of temperatures.

Drinking a gallon of coffee or gulping a few energy drinks might seem like a great idea, but it is, in fact, a very bad one. Caffeine, pep pills or other artificial sources of energy are more likely to leave you feeling rushed and ragged. Your brain might be clicking along, all right, but chances are good it is not clicking along on the right track! Furthermore, drinking coffee or energy drinks will mean frequent trips to the rest room. This will cut into the time you should be spending answering questions and is a distraction in itself, since each time you need to leave the room you lose focus. Pep pills will only make it harder for you to think straight when solving complicated problems.

At the same time, if anxiety is your problem try to find ways around using tranquilizers during test-taking time. Even medically prescribed anti-anxiety medication can make you less alert and even decrease your motivation. Being motivated is what you need to get you through an exam. If your anxiety is so bad that it threatens to interfere with your ability to take an exam, speak to your doctor and ask for documentation. Many testing sites will allow non-distracting test rooms, extended testing time and other accommodations with a doctor's note that explains the situation is made available.

Keep Breathing.

It might not make a lot of sense, but when people become anxious, tense, or scared, their breathing becomes shallow and, sometimes stop breathing all together! Pay attention to your emotions, and when you are feeling worried, focus on your breathing. Take a moment to remind yourself to breathe deeply and regularly. Drawing in steady, deep breaths energizes the body. When you continue to breathe deeply you will notice you exhale all the tension.

If you feel you need to, try rehearsing breathing at home. With continued practice of this relaxation technique, you will begin to know the muscles that tense up under pressure. Call these your "signal muscles." These are the ones that will speak to you first, begging you to relax. Take the time to listen to those muscles and do as they ask. With just a little breathing practice, you will get into the habit of checking yourself regularly and when you realize you are tense, relaxation will become second nature.

AVOID ANXIETY BEFORE A TEST

Manage your time effectively.

This is a key to your success! You need blocks of uninterrupted time to study all the pertinent material. Creating and maintaining a schedule will help keep you on track, and will remind family members and friends that you are not available. Under no circumstances should you change your blocks of study time to accommodate someone else, or cancel a study session to do something more fun. Do not interfere with your study time for any reason!

Relax.

Use whatever works best for you to relieve stress. Some folks like a good, calming stretch with yoga, others find expressing themselves through journaling to be useful. Some hit the floor for a series of crunches or planks, and still others take a slow stroll around the garden. Integrate a little relaxation time into your schedule, and treat that time, too, as sacred.

Eat healthy.

Instead of reaching for the chips and chocolate, fresh fruits and vegetables are not only yummy but offer nutritional benefits that help to relieve stress. Some foods accelerate stress instead of reducing it and should be avoided. Foods that add to higher anxiety include artificial sweeteners, candy and other sugary foods, carbonated sodas, chips, chocolate, eggs, fried foods, junk foods, processed foods, red meat, and other foods containing preservatives or heavy spices. Instead, eat a bowl of berries and some yogurt!

Get plenty of ZZZZZZZs.

Do not cram or try to do an all-nighter. If you created a study schedule at the beginning, and if you have stuck with that schedule, have confidence! Staying up too late trying to cram in last-minute bits of information is going to leave you exhausted the next day. Besides, whatever new information you cram in will only displace all the important ideas you've spent weeks learning. Remember: You need to be alert and fully functional the day of the exam

Have confidence in yourself!

Everyone experiences some anxiety when taking a test, but exhibiting a positive attitude banishes anxiety and fills you with the knowledge you really do know what you need to know. This is your opportunity to show how well prepared you are. Go for it!

Be sure to take everything you need.

Depending on the exam, you may be allowed to have a pen or pencil, calculator, dictionary or scratch paper with you. Have these gathered together along with your entrance paperwork and identification so that you are sure you have everything that is needed.

Do not chitchat with friends.

Let your friends know ahead of time that it is not anything personal, but you are going to ignore them in the test room! You need to find a seat away from doors and windows, one that has good lighting, and get comfortable. If other students are worried their anxiety could be detrimental to you; of course, you do not have to tell your friends that. If you are afraid they will be offended, tell them you are protecting them from your anxiety!

COMMON TEST-TAKING MISTAKES

Taking a test is not much fun at best. When you take a test and make a stupid mistake that negatively affects your grade, it is natural to be very upset, especially when it is something that could have been easily avoided. So what are some of the common mistakes that are made on tests?

Put your name on the test!.

How could you possibly forget to put your name on a test? You would be amazed at how often that happens. Very often, tests without names are thrown out immediately, resulting in a failing grade.

How to Take a Test

Marking the wrong multiple-choice answer.

It is important to work at a steady pace, but that does not mean bolting through the questions. Be sure the answer you are marking is the one you mean to. If the bubble you need to fill in or the answer you need to circle is 'C', do not allow yourself to get distracted and select 'B' instead.

Answering a question twice.

Some multiple-choice test questions have two very similar answers. If you are in too much of a hurry, you might select them both. Remember that only one answer is correct, so if you choose more than one, you have automatically failed that question.

Mishandling a difficult question.

We recommend skipping difficult questions and returning to them later, but beware! First, be certain that you do return to the question. Circling the entire passage or placing a large question mark beside it will help you spot it when you are reviewing your test. Secondly, if you are not careful to skip the question, you can mess yourself up badly. Imagine that a question is too difficult and you decide to save it for later. You read the next question, which you know the answer to, and you fill in that answer. You continue to the end of the test then return to the difficult question only to discover you didn't actually skip it! Instead, you inserted the answer to the following question in the spot reserved for the harder one, thus throwing off the remainder of your test!

Incorrectly Transferring an answer from scratch paper.

This can happen easily if you are trying to hurry! Double check any answer you have figured out on scratch paper, and make sure what you have written on the test itself is an exact match!

Don't ignore the clock, and don't marry it, either.

In a timed examination many students lose track of the time and end up without sufficient time to complete the test. Remember to pace yourself! At the same time, though, do not allow yourself to become obsessed with how much time has elapsed, either.

Thinking too much.

Generally, your first thought is your best thought. If you worry yourself into insecurity, your self-doubts can trick you into choosing an incorrect answer when your first impulse was the right one!

Conclusion

CONGRATULATIONS! You have made it this far because you have applied yourself diligently to practicing for the exam and no doubt improved your potential score considerably! Getting into a good school is a huge step in a journey that might be challenging at times but will be many times more rewarding and fulfilling. That is why being prepared is so important.

Good Luck!

Register for Free Updates and More Practice Test Questions

Register your purchase at https://www.test-preparation.ca/register/

for updates, free test tips and more practice test questions.

ONLINE RESOURCES

How to Prepare for a Test - The Ultimate Guide

https://www.test-preparation.ca/prepare-test/

Learning Styles - The Complete Guide

https://www.test-preparation.ca/learning-style/

Test Anxiety Secrets!

https://www.test-preparation.ca/test-anxiety/

Time Management on a Test

https://www.test-preparation.ca/time-management/

Flash Cards - The Complete Guide

https://www.test-preparation.ca/flash-cards/

Test Preparation Video Series

https://www.test-preparation.ca/test-video/

How to Memorize - The Complete Guide

https://www.test-preparation.ca/memorize/

Online Library of Student Tips and Strategies

https://www.test-preparation.ca/students-say/

CORRECTIONS SITUATION JUDGEMENT

Mathematics

Corrections Situation Judgement

MATHEMATICS

CORRECTIONS SITUATION JUDGEMENT

Mathematics

Corrections Situation Judgement

Mathematics

CONCLUSION

CONGRATULATIONS! You have made it this far because you have applied yourself diligently to practicing for the exam and no doubt improved your potential score considerably! Getting into a good school is a huge step in a journey that might be challenging at times but will be many times more rewarding and fulfilling. That is why being prepared is so important.

Study then Practice and then Succeed!

Good Luck!

Mathematics

CORRECTIONS SITUATION JUDGEMENT

ONLINE RESOURCES

How to Prepare for a Test - The Ultimate Guide

https://www.test-preparation.ca/the-ultimate-guide-to-test-preparation-strategy/

Learning Styles - The Complete Guide

https://www.test-preparation.ca/learning-styles/

Test Anxiety Secrets!

https://www.test-preparation.ca/how-to-overcome-test-anxiety/

Time Management on a Test

https://www.test-preparation.ca/test-tactics-the-time-wise-approach/

Flash Cards - The Complete Guide

https://www.test-preparation.ca/test-preparation-with-flash-cards/

Test Preparation Video Series

https://www.test-preparation.ca/video-series-on-test-preparation-multiple-choice-strategies-and-how-to-study/

How to Memorize - The Complete Guide

https://www.test-preparation.ca/a-guide-to-memorizing-anything-easily-and-painlessly/

MATHEMATICS

www.ingramcontent.com/pod-product-compliance
Lightning Source LLC
LaVergne TN
LVHW010302260326
834688LV00044B/1413